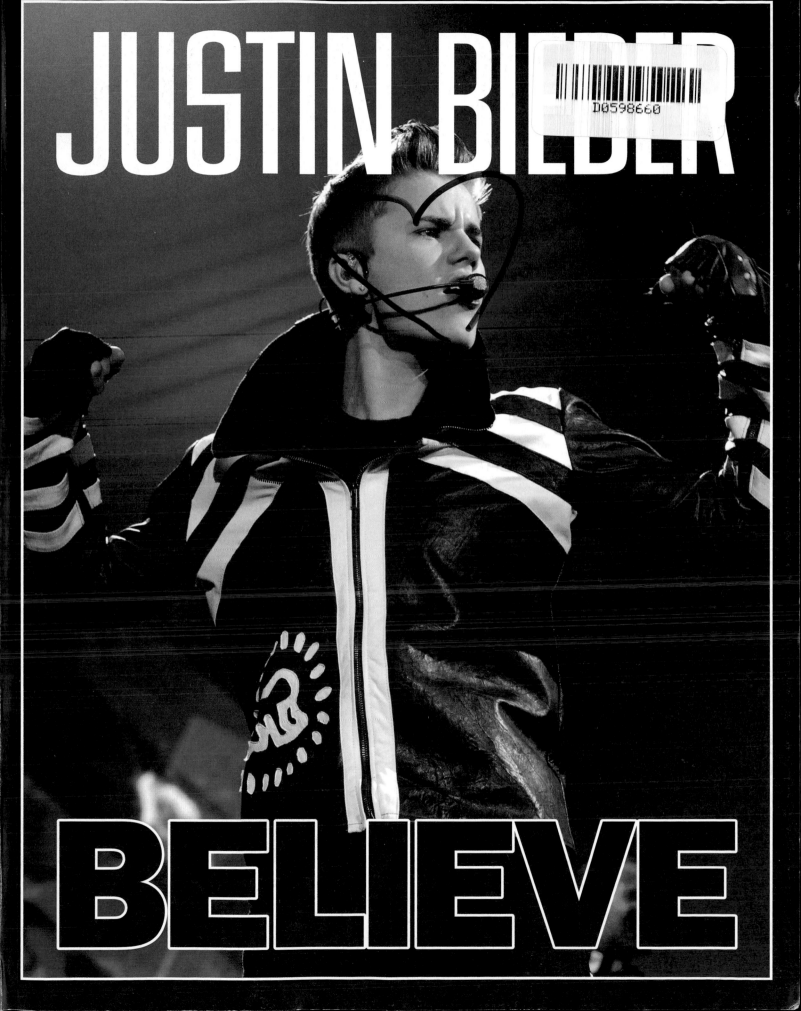

JUSTIN BIEBER

BELIEVE

This book is available in quantity at special discounts for your group or organization. For further information, contact:

Triumph Books LLC
814 North Franklin Street
Chicago, Illinois 60610
Phone: (312) 337-0747

www.triumphbooks.com

Printed in U.S.A.
ISBN: 978-1-60078-792-8

Content packaged by Mojo Media, Inc.
Joe Funk: Editor
Jason Hinman: Creative Director

All photos courtesy of Getty Images unless otherwise noted.

Contents

Justin At 18!

Above: While he's certainly not a fighter, Justin Bieber is a heavyweight champion when it comes to being a 21st century, multimedia, pop culture superstar. Opposite: Justin laid low on his actual 18th birthday, preferring to spend the day with loved ones and trying to organize another Twitter charity campaign. He was not forgotten by his fans, however, as this huge Bieber fan excitedly reveals an updated wax figure of Justin at Madame Tussaud's in Hollywood on March 1. There is also a pair of Bieber waxes in Europe, making Justin one of the most popular celebrities to be depicted in wax.

He's sold over 8 million records, been nominated for a pair of Grammys, and boasts one of the largest and most devoted fan bases in the world. He has donated more money to charity than nearly any other celebrity, and he's just turned 18. No, Justin Bieber is not a typical 18 year old, not by a long shot. He's one of the most famous people in the world and has remained humble despite his success, a true underdog that has become a superstar.

Since becoming internationally famous three years ago, Bieber's active life has forced him to grow up faster than most teenagers. With the support of a great network of business partners and a wonderful family influence, however, Biebs was able to ring in his 18th birthday as a well-balanced, kind-hearted star in a world filled with celebrities behaving badly.

When he turned 17 on March 1, 2011, Justin focused his energy on one of the things that he does best: his charity

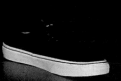

work. Using the power of his Twitter army of Beliebers, Justin spent the day raising money for the organization charity: water, a cause close to his heart. He urged his followers to donate $17, in the end garnering over $47,000 for the charity. With his 18th birthday approaching, Justin wanted to do something special for charity again. He Tweeted messages about other charities in addition to charity: water, guiding them to donate to several worthy causes. It's a classic Justin moment, taking the spotlight off of himself to raise tens of thousands of dollars for great causes.

Justin received a special birthday present from his manager, Scooter Braun, during an appearance on Ellen DeGeneres' television show, a $100,000 Fisker Karma electric car. The vehicle is extremely eco-friendly, with all of the wood trim coming from trees that fell on their own and surfaces made of fabrics that feature no animal products. The swanky new wheels are ultra-rare and set Justin apart from the pack. He was certainly surprised by the awesome gift!

It's been a while since Justin has been on tour but he has spent lots of time performing whenever he gets the chance. Even if he only gets to sing a song or two, it's always worth it for Justin to stretch his voice and let his fans see what he does best: perform.

Even though he's already crossed over into being an international superstar, 2012 might be the year that Justin truly conquers the music business. His bangs are gone and he's 18 now, focused not only on keeping his fans happy but making new fans as well.

Part of the hype for releasing a new album is making media appearances. Justin is a natural on the interview circuit and always has new bits of information to drop when he talks to the media.

Justin is quickly becoming a fixture on MTV. After winning awards on both sides of the Atlantic, he's moved into a part-time hosting gig on the network's legendary prank show Punk'd.

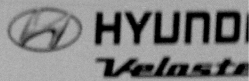

EMA
BELFAST 2011

DELL

The power to do more

Braun mentioned that even though Justin does not usually have flashy things like exotic cars, he'd have to make an exception for the awesome new ride.

Meanwhile, Justin splurged on a special gift for himself, reportedly buying a mansion in Los Angeles for $10.8 million. A former home of Ashton Kutcher, the house in the Hollywood Hills comes in at a huge 9,400 square feet and includes five bedrooms, retractable glass walls, a gourmet kitchen, a gym, and a massage room. After all of his hard work and tireless work on behalf of those less fortunate, Justin finally has a place to call home at the end of the day when he wants to kick his feet up.

All in all, Justin has accomplished way more than the average 18 year old. As a legal adult, he has access to his full fortune, estimated at over $100,000,000! In just a few short years he has gone from singing at home to worldwide superstardom, and as any Bieber fan can attest, it couldn't have happened to a better guy. How did he cap off his birthday? Justin took a minute on Ellen to announce a

Not only did Justin win the award for Favorite Singer at the Kids' Choice Awards, he was presented with his orange blimp by good friend Jaden Smith. The pair shared a salute and a hug on stage when Justin's name was announced.

With his new album just about ready to be released, Justin spent most of the spring getting ready for it to drop. This has meant lots of studio work and plenty of promotional work, including interviews with the media from far and wide.

One of the places where Justin is most popular—even compared to usual—is France. Earlier this year he took the time to take home an award at the NRJ Music Awards, stealing the show with his kind-hearted words of victory delivered on-stage in French.

A perfectly captured moment as Justin reacts to the first bits of slime hitting him at the Nickelodeon Kids' Choice Awards. Justin has been a mainstay at the awards since his career began and has frequently taken home orange blimps from the ceremony.

Justin took home some hardware from the Tribeca Disruptive Innovation Awards in April, showing off his latest haircut. Commenting about his new album, Justin informed fans that they have lots to look forward to in 2012.

TRIBECA
FILM
FESTIVAL.
AMERICAN EXPRESS
FOUNDING SPONSOR

NEW YORK UNIVERSITY
NYU
STERN
LEONARD N. STERN
SCHOOL OF BUSINESS

new single, "Boyfriend," that was released later in the month.

With a new album due to drop in June, Justin Bieber is at the top of the world at 18. There's no doubt that he's about to sell millions of records in 2012 and maintain his spot as one of the most popular singing stars in the world. The last few years have been amazing; the next few are about to be even better.

Above: Before he was slimed later that night, Justin wows the crowd at the Kids' Choice Awards in Los Angeles. Justin's fan support has never been higher, peaking at a perfect time before the new album. Opposite: Justin and Selena can be frequently spotted around L.A. while they both are hard at work on their 2012 projects. They like to take time out for dates, including going to Lakers games. They were once featured on the Kiss Cam, a moment Selena calls one of the most embarrassing of her life.

New Album!

Above: A talented musician, Justin has looked forward to the new album to show off more of his songwriting abilities. The new songs that have been heard by certain people in the music business have all met with good reviews. Opposite: Justin has been ramping up his celebrity appearances in anticipation of the new album, and one man he has been seen with lately is Will Ferrell. The two always combine for hilarious moments, so seeing them out together may result in something new and exciting.

Set to hit store shelves on June 19, Justin Bieber's *Believe* is likely to be the biggest record of 2012. While that might sound like a bold prediction, it would just be another hit entry in Justin's catalog. He has topped the sales charts before and based on his fans' response to the early releases from *Believe,* Justin is as good as ever on his new record.

Most of the album was recorded with Justin's team in L.A., though he has spent time recording with famed producer Timbaland to revise his sound slightly. With a bit more rap and more of a club sound than his previous albums, Justin's new effort reflects how the singer has matured as a person and an artist.

In the weeks and months leading up to the album's release, there were several reports anticipating *Believe's* unique sound. The most obvious hint is in the album's first single,

"Boyfriend." Released digitally in March and then featured during an appearance on *The Voice* in April, the video for the song was released in early May alongside the single.

With a new R&B and hip hop sound to it, "Boyfriend" is still a pop hit but it sounds different than most of Justin's earlier work, drawing comparisons to Justin Timberlake. Critics enjoyed the new sound from the start, saying that it shows that Justin Bieber is willing to grow up with his music as he grows up himself.

The song was an immediate smash hit, hitting the top spot in the iTunes store within hours of its release. Immediately, music industry insiders wondered where it would debut on the Billboard charts. It seemed like the Top 5—and a new career high—was easily within reach, but could Justin debut at No. 1 for his first chart-topping song in the United States?

In its first week, "Boyfriend" sold 521,000 digital copies, earning it the No. 2 spot on the Billboard

As Justin has gotten older, his voice has changed slightly. He has said that he has to sing some songs, like "Baby," in a different key than they were written because he can't hit all of the same notes he used to. The changes have opened up totally new keys to him, however, and it will be exciting to hear the changes on *Believe.*

Justin performs with an old friend, Sean Kingston. There are several guests confirmed for the new album, perfect for Justin since so many of his previous tracks have been remixed and since he has been appearing as a guest on several other artists' tracks.

Fans can look forward to a new tour in support of the album and expect more moments like this at every show. This lucky fan not only was serenaded, she received a dozen roses from Justin.

Hot 100 for its debut. It was the highest chart position of Justin's career and No. 1 would have been in sight, though the song missed out on the top spot since it was only available on iTunes and through no other retailer. The song did, however, come out at No. 1 in the country nearest and dearest to Justin's heart: Canada.

"Boyfriend" became Justin's biggest hit ever in the first week of its release, but what about the rest of the album? This spring, dozens of music journalists were invited to a listening party in London that featured eight songs off the new album and a question-and-answer session with Bieber. The songs, by all accounts, sounded like ready-made hits for the car or the club. Anticipation was beginning to build as presales began for the album, all but assuring it the top spot on Billboard's album chart the week it is released.

It's not just Bieber providing the vocals on *Believe*. The single for "Boyfriend" features collaborator Mike Posner and several songs will feature other star artists. Kanye West, who has remixed

Justin has been popular on the radio scene lately, dropping in on studios all over the country to talk about his new album and give more inside information on the story behind his new single, "Boyfriend."

Justin's songs before, and longtime friend Taylor Swift are two of the people believed to have collaborated on songs that will be included on *Believe.*

There has been a late entry to Justin's song catalog, though it is unclear whether the song will be part of the new album. "Turn to You," a tribute to Justin's mom Pattie, was announced in the build up to Mother's Day 2012, with all proceeds going to charity.

No album is more anticipated in 2012 than *Believe.* All but guaranteed to be one of the best albums of the year, Beliebers can take heart in the fact that even though Justin's sound is maturing a bit, the same catchy, awesome personality that has made Justin such a superstar is still alive and well. All early indications are that 2012 will truly be the year of Bieber.

Justin's new album will provide opportunities to do work benefiting his favorite charitable causes. In November 2011, he posed alongside members of the Marine Corps Toys for Tots program at New York's Empire State Building and encouraged his fans to donate toys for less fortunate children that holiday season.

In a rare opening role, Justin performs with rapper Lil' Twist in support of TYGA. Justin is stretching his musical voice on the new album, with more hip hop meaning that he's had to practice his rapping whenever he gets a chance.

With the new tour that will come in support of the album, fans can expect a new stage show from Justin. After all the magic of his last world tour, it will be amazing to see what's in store for the next one.

Perhaps the best entertainer of this decade, Justin is one of music's biggest superstars thanks to his incredible sound and army of fans. The Beliebers make Justin who he is, and he'll never forget that as he dedicates every show to them.

The Women In His Life

AP Images

Above: One of the most important ladies in Justin's life is also the smallest. Justin's sister Jazmyn seems to love the spotlight, and she often comes on stage to sing with her brother to her favorite song, "Baby." Opposite: It's easy to look good next to such a pretty girl, but Justin and Selena manage to take it to another level when it's time to walk the red carpet. The pair are one of Hollywood's hottest couples.

Justin wouldn't be where he is today without the influence of many people, but it might be the women in his life who have shaped him more than anyone else. His mom, Pattie, raised Justin to be the person he is today and is easily the most important influence on Justin's life.

When Justin was born, Pattie knew she was probably going to have to raise him on her own after she and Jeremy Bieber split up. She had the help of her parents and began to work hard at office jobs, earning enough money to keep her and her son afloat in Statford's lower-income housing neighborhoods. She scratched and clawed to provide a life for her young son, rising above the tough circumstances to create a happy family. Justin has always idolized his mom for what she did for him, calling her the biggest reason for his success.

It was Pattie, of course, who first wanted to show off Justin's singing talent and created a YouTube account to do it. The videos were posted by a proud mom just wanting to share Justin with family and friends, but they were incredibly popular and the key to the start of Justin's career.

For Mother's Day in 2012 Justin showed just how dedicated he is to his mom, releasing a new tribute song called "Turn To You," an emotional track about how much Pattie has supported him in life. The proceeds benefit charities that help out other single moms. Pattie is starting to carve a larger public image for herself and plans on releasing a book in the fall of 2012, a memoir about what is was like raising her famous son all on her own and all of the pressures that went with it.

Of course, being a young, successful, good-looking singer in the public eye means earning the attention of lots of girls. Justin has always been a romantic at heart, looking for one person

It's easy to love such a wonderful lady. Justin has never been shy about his love for his mom, frequently talking about how much he loves and respects the woman who raised him on his own. Justin's new single, written about his mom, will benefit charities that help single mothers.

Justin had a great date to his first Grammy Awards, his stunning mom, Pattie. When Justin began in the music business his mom was his guiding influence, making sure he didn't get in over his head or associate with bad people. She's Justin's rock, and always will be.

Pattie loves any chance to walk the red carpet with her son and couldn't have been more proud than she was at his movie premiere. She made every first showing of his film, including the European debut and the New York premiere of the 3D version of Never Say Never.

to truly love. It looks like he may have already found her. Actress and singer Selena Gomez, who rocketed to fame as the star of "Wizards of Waverly Place," caught Justin's attention in 2010. As a busy star herself, Selena understood the trials of living life as a famous young person and the pair hit it off.

The beautiful brunette is two years older than Justin and is considered a true Hollywood fashionista, one of the most stylish ladies in town. She's been instrumental to Justin's new grown-up look, which has been apparent in recent months when he has dressed up to walk the red carpet.

The pair began dating in 2010 but didn't publicly admit their relationship until the Oscars at the end of February 2011, instantly making them one of the hottest celebrity couples. Justin is the romantic of the pair, loving to make dramatic gestures for his leading lady. The pair have been spotted on trips in Hawaii and Mexico, on cute dates around L.A., and she has even dropped by the

Justin's whole clan rarely gets the chance to appear together, so the moments they do get to spend together are cherished. Justin's mom and dad may have split up years ago, but they are both proud of their son. One of Justin's favorite people in the world is his sister Jazmyn, the daughter of his dad.

Though Justin will always be most comfortable in a hoodie, part of being a legal adult is now dressing the part. In addition to his ever-changing haircuts, Justin is now being seen in more formal wear, especially when awards shows call for him to dress up. Selena has no problems getting her guy into a tux, and Justin might look better than ever in a black tie.

sets of Justin's music videos to spend some quality time with her guy. They really are a cute couple!

Of course, Justin's mother and girlfriend aren't the only influential women in his life. Don't forget about his little sister Jazmyn, a little firecracker who absolutely adores her big brother. There are a pair of important ladies in his professional inner circle, too—his tutor Jenny has helped him stay on track with his studies on the road while vocal coach "Mama" Jan Smith, one of the music industry's most respected teachers, has helped him perfect his craft.

Justin and his mom, accompanied by Scooter Braun, put on quite the show at the Grammys last year. Even though Justin didn't take home an award, winning a Grammy is at the top of his list of goals.

In addition to his tutor, Jenny, Justin spends lots of time with members of his entourage that are women. One of the most important is "Mama" Jan Smith, a well-respected vocal coach that took Justin under her wing. Now, Justin can step up to any mic with no warm-up and deliver pitch-perfect singing.

Justin's mom is probably able to tell the difference between her son and his wax figure since the two are so inseparable. She has remained an active but behind-the-scenes mom, allowing her son to grow as an artist but always staying close enough so the pair can frequently have dinner and spend time together.

Before they became a couple, Justin and Selena were already inseparable as friends. This fueled speculation that the two would hook up, though they both managed to downplay it and keep things quiet for several months.

One of Justin's earliest career connections was Usher. Naturally, he was one of the first to meet Selena when she and Justin first got together. They're all seen here backstage at an awards ceremony in Atlanta.

Biggest Influences

Opposite: Of all the places to run into pal Ludacris, the CMT Music Awards in Nashville is not the most likely. It was at the country music awards show, though, that Justin ran into his partner from his breakout hit, "Baby."

Every musical artist has influences that help define his or her unique sound. Justin Bieber has managed to take the voices of those who came before him to create a sound all his own, blending classic pop elements with R&B and some rap to make his own distinct brand of music.

Justin grew up listening to all sorts of music thanks to his parents' diverse musical interests, so there was never anything off-limits to Justin's ears. He heard everything from hard rock to hip hop to gospel, learning to appreciate the talents of artists of all kinds. His tastes are ever-changing, so his answers to the question of his musical influences have varied at different points in his career.

There are a few artists, however, who have had more of an impact on Justin than others. One is one of music's biggest voices ever, Stevie Wonder. Justin has long admired Wonder's sound and stage presence, and was humbled when he got to

RESPONSE

share the stage with one of his idols in late 2011 on *The X Factor*. Listening to the pair's duet made it easy to see why Justin calls him a major influence on his voice.

As a musician, Justin is a talented guitar player and a respected drummer, interests forged by the rock and roll tastes of his dad, Jeremy. Artists like Jimi Hendrix captivated Justin with their mastery of guitar, making the instrument an extension of themselves.

Of course, one of the biggest influences on Justin's career is close friend Usher. The super-famous singer has been a top-selling artist for more than 10 years and knows all about life at the top of the charts. Like Justin, Usher burst onto the scene seemingly out of nowhere, though he is always fast to point out that Justin rose to fame much quicker than he did. Justin values Usher's presence in his life as a mentor because Usher has been in his shoes.

Usher helps keep Justin grounded after all of his success, helps him manage career challenges like changing his sound, has helped Justin with his fan

Performing with legends is a great part of the job of being a superstar. Justin made an appearance on Fox's *The X Factor* in late 2011 and had a chance to sing a pair of duets with one of the men who influenced his singing voice, Stevie Wonder.

After meeting in Atlanta through Scooter Braun, Justin and Usher quickly became inseparable. The older singer sees a lot of himself in Justin, and tries to help steer him in the right direction.

At Christmastime Justin likes to appear with his friends to celebrate the holiday spirit. He appeared on NBC's Today alongside Usher in 2011 to ring in the start of the season.

relations, and basically serves as a guide to what to do and what not to do in the music business. Though his mom and Scooter Braun probably have a bigger impact on Justin in his everyday life, Usher is the man who has seen it all and been where Justin has been.

As a pop singer, Justin cannot help but be influenced by the King of Pop, Michael Jackson. A star as a child in the Jackson 5 in the 1970s, Jackson broke out as the biggest pop star ever in the 1980s with his record-breaking, history-making album *Thriller*. The benchmark for every pop singer who followed, Jackson influenced countless artists. Bieber spoke at an event honoring Jackson in early 2012, talking about what a trailblazer the singer had been.

Another one of his influences has helped bring a decidedly R&B sound into Justin's music: Boyz II Men. The popular 1990s singing group lends a part of their sound to Justin's songs, with their influence on Justin's voice giving it a soul power that many are surprised to hear out of an 18-year-old singer.

One of the biggest influences on Justin's sound is the popular 1990s group Boyz II Men. The group had some of the biggest crossover hits of the decade and their smooth sound, friendly attitudes, and awesome live show have inspired Justin his entire career. He performed with them in 2010.

The mentor and the student pose with their American Music Awards in 2010. Justin took home four wins that night and invited Usher on stage with him, saying he felt he had to pay homage to someone that affected him so much. It was a night of celebration for the pair as they couldn't help but smile widely.

AMERICAN M

ARDS

AMERICAN MUSIC AWARD

One common characteristic among Justin's musical influences is their ability to entertain a crowd, something that Justin has said he holds dear. He realizes that his music, like his influences', is all about entertaining those who love listening to it. With friendly, giving personalities and incredible live acts, all of Justin's main influences have shown Justin the importance of being humble and then going on stage and giving the fans exactly what they want to see.

Above: It was a holiday special on NBC's Today when Usher and Justin performed together in a rare duet. The pair sounded so natural together it wouldn't be surprising to see them pair up again! Opposite: Alongside Michael Jackson's children and brother Jermaine, Justin poses for a picture at the Michael Jackson "Immortalized" hand and footprint ceremony in January 2012. With his keynote speech, Justin was able to perfectly capture what made Jackson the immortal "King of Pop."

Looking sharp in their 3D glasses, Usher and Scooter Braun take in the premiere of *Never Say Never* in Los Angeles alongside Justin. His two closest mentors are also two of his closest friends.

His Hobbies

Above: Justin loves to skateboard when he has the chance and featured the sport in his video for "One Time." That board was autographed and preserved by the Hard Rock Café, who sent the skateboard out on a memorabilia tour in 2011. Opposite: Justin feels right at home with a basketball in his hands when an errant pass comes his way during an NBA game. He is a shifty guard who likes to play whenever possible, occasionally against some awesome competition.

Since he's an international superstar with millions of albums sold and one of the largest fan bases in the world, it's easy to forget sometimes that Justin Bieber is just a regular teenager. Until March 2012, he was still just a kid. Like any guy his age, Justin has hobbies. Unsurprisingly, many of them are pretty normal.

Justin's biggest hobby is playing sports. Even though he's a smaller guy, he loves competing in just about anything and sports are a perfect way to blow off some steam. He's played a variety of sports and he's super athletic, making him a natural at just about anything.

Since he's Canadian, Justin's first sports love was undoubtedly hockey. Even though it's a tough, physical sport, smaller guys like Justin with a big heart can have lots of success just like he did. As a child, Justin was named

The Dallas Mavericks' Dirk Nowitzki towers over Justin at the 2011 ESPYs. The pair first met when Justin attended the NBA Finals, where Dirk carried the Mavs to a championship.

The Los Angeles Kings have quite the celebrity following, especially among Canadians. Justin is an avid fan and has been spotted at several games.

team captain more than once for his leadership abilities and he's a smooth skater with a good head for the game.

When he was granting a wish to a sick child in 2011, Justin knew it was a perfect chance to lace up his skates with members of his favorite team, the Toronto Maple Leafs. Several Leafs players, including captain and Canadian international player Dion Phaneuf, met with Bieber and eight-year-old Jake Schafer for a day of playing. Justin donned a full Leafs track suit and looked good on the ice, not even a bit rusty as he went up against the pros. He showed off his smooth skating and lots of shifty moves, scoring some neat goals.

Justin's combination of small size, speed, and quick moves is what makes him such a dangerous athlete. During a European tour he decided to try another of his favorite sports, soccer. Whenever he is back home in Stratford Justin likes to lace up his boots and play in a league with some of his closest friends, so it was only natural when he went to Europe that he would take the field alongside the

It's always been said that Justin is at his sporting best on the ice; it's in his blood. As a small, speedy player, Justin excels in sports where he can be let loose to go as fast as he can—opponents usually can't keep up with his quickness.

world's most popular sport's top professional players.

During a tour stop in Spain Justin took a chance to visit with one of the most successful teams in the world, Barcelona. He was given a full practice uniform and sent out with the team for training, putting on a fine performance. After doing some media appearances, Justin took to the streets in his gear, playing a game of street soccer that showcased his skills.

When his tour took him to England, Justin visited Chelsea FC in London for a day with one of the Premier League's top teams. This time wearing a full uniform from the "Blues," Justin took to the pitch at Stamford Bridge with two of the top players in the world, Frank Lampard and Fernando Torres. Justin's booming free kicks drew a great response from the normally tough English media.

Back at home, one of Justin's most significant breaks into mainstream America's consciousness came as a result

Justin doesn't get to spend much time back home in Stratford, but he loves cutting loose and having fun whenever he does get back. One of his hobbies is playing on a soccer team with his childhood friends.

of his love for sports. The 2011 NBA All-Star Game was held in Los Angeles and the NBA organized a celebrity game filled with old pros, current WNBA players, actors, and musicians. It ended up being one of the most popular events of the weekend.

Justin was playing on a team with close friend and collaborator Romeo Miller, a former player at USC. The pair stole the show, with Justin burning by actor Michael Rappaport, proving to be too much for Common's attempted defense, and even swiping the ball from Hall of Famer Scottie Pippen. Justin was the hit of the night, earning MVP honors and a standing ovation from the fans.

At the end of the day, Justin really is just a regular teenager who loves to play. He also golfs and rides skateboards. All in all, Justin is a normal guy who gets the chance to do some really cool things that most sports fans can only dream of. He's such a good athlete, maybe he'll end up with a second career playing something professionally one day!

His soccer training session with Barcelona was much more intense than the one with Chelsea Here, Justin works on Bojan Krkic, one of the best young players in the world. Justin wasn't just there to snap a few pictures, he had to earn his spot on the pitch.

Funniest Moments

Above: With a grueling schedule in December before the holidays, Justin had to take some time out to be silly and make some laughs when he was appearing on NBC's Today. Opposite: A Nickelodeon tradition as Biebs and Kids' Choice Awards Host Will Smith react to their sliming at the 25th annual awards show. Bieber should have known this was coming, since it was Canadian show You Can't Do That On Television that started Nickelodeon's sliming ways in the 1990s.

Ask anyone who knows Justin Bieber about his sense of humor and the stories will start pouring out almost immediately. A joker and a prankster, Justin is famous for his wicked sense of timing and great jokes. Still, his humor can get him into trouble sometimes, and those around him are always looking for an opportunity to get some laughs at his expense.

Justin is well-known for acting silly, as his team of people knows very well. He is always playing little jokes on people in the studio or while traveling, keeping the mood light. Surrounded by so many business-oriented grown-ups, it's certainly appreciated that Justin can make everyone smile.

Of course, part of having a sense of humor is being able to laugh at oneself. All it takes is one look at some of Justin's outlandish comedy outfits or seeing him read David

Letterman's Top Ten List about himself to realize that Justin has no problem laughing when the joke's on him. Then again, that segment started with a classic Justin quip, implying that he has no idea who the famous late-night talk show host is.

Justin and Will Smith fell to one of the oldest pranks in the book at the Kids' Choice Awards this year. Nickelodeon's famous slime, a mainstay of the network for over 20 years, found Bieber and the host of the show while they spoke at the podium, covering them both in the green goo that had the crowd rolling with laughter.

Outside of awards shows, Justin likes to shake things up from time to time, wearing costumes and walking around with a microphone to interview celebrities. Though his fake mustaches, huge glasses, and funny hats do little to trick the celebrities he interviews, they love playing along with his questions, which are usually just about some guy named Justin Bieber.

Justin is one of the most famous users on Twitter,

Wearing a mustache to "hide" his identity, Justin interviews actor Jeremy Renner on the red carpet of the Critics' Choice Movie Awards in 2011. With his glasses and mustache fooling no one, he asked actors like Renner and Elle Fanning if they'd ever heard of this new singer named, of course, Justin Bieber.

During a lighthearted moment at the Teen Choice Awards in 2011, Taylor Swift takes a minute to get close to her good friend. There was little smiling in 2012, however, when Justin made Taylor his victim on the new version of MTV's *Punk'd*. Justin made Taylor cry, though they have since made up and are as close as ever.

Comedic actors have recognized Justin's natural humor from the start of his career. Legendary comedian Adam Sandler is among the many professionals who finds Justin hilarious.

responsible for three percent of the company's server usage. His more than 20 million Beliebers make up one of the most expansive Twitter armies ever assembled, and they often get to see Justin's sense of humor come through in his Tweets.

Manager Scooter Braun is a frequent target of Justin's, with the singer softly ribbing Scooter for taking an extra 15 minutes for his lunch. His own music takes a hit, with Justin expressing mock surprise that no one got the meaning of "Boyfriend," which he claimed is about bird migration. Justin makes references to his favorite movies and singers, gets in on inside jokes with his fans, and generally has a great time with his Twitter humor.

Justin really was a natural, then, to take over MTV's *Punk'd*. The series had once been one of the network's most popular shows when it was hosted by Ashton Kutcher, featuring a series of pranks played on other celebrities. Since Justin is well-known for playing pranks on his friends and definitely

Justin makes a reference to the movie *Talladega Nights* while presenting an award with Danica Patrick at the 2011 ESPYs. The popular race car driver passed on wearing a fireproof racing suit to dress up like the other attendees, but Justin had to have a laugh and wear the full garb, much to the delight of Danica and the crowd.

comfortable in front of a camera, MTV approached him about hosting a new version of the series. Justin declined the full-time job, but instead took the helm for two episodes of the new season.

Some of Justin's targets included skateboarder Rob Dyrdek (who might have figured out the punking), Miley Cyrus, and his good friend Taylor Swift. He got Swift too well, however, making the singer cry when she thought she had ruined someone's dream wedding. The country singer got the last laugh, however, when she pranked Justin with a phone call about a fake lawsuit a few weeks later. It was all in good fun, and when Justin realized it was Taylor behind the fake call, they all had a good laugh.

Justin realizes the importance of keeping things lighthearted from time to time. The entertainment business is a hard one to succeed in, so being able to take a minute to smile and laugh helps make life just a little bit easier for everyone. His guest spots in sketches on

There might not be a more charming late night talk show guest than Justin. He has made appearances on just about every network late night show, and though he might have a favorite among them, he makes every host laugh whenever he appears. Here, he has television legend David Letterman cracking up.

shows like *Saturday Night Live* and the website FunnyOrDie.com reveal that Justin has some expert comedic timing, making his already humorous dialogue absolutely hilarious.

He's one funny guy. Justin's sense of humor is becoming famous in Hollywood and one person who has certainly taken notice is his girlfriend, Selena. She frequently comments on how much she enjoys Justin's sense of humor and jokes, saying that she is lucky to be with such a free spirit. Justin's funny moments bring out smiles for everyone, and that might be the most important thing.

Above: A close collaborator of Justin's on many web projects, Will Ferrell is one of the funniest people alive. He can't help but laugh at one of Justin's jokes. Opposite: Justin struts his stuff on the red carpet with another Canadian in glasses, comedic actor Seth Rogen.

A Worldwide Sensation

Above: European TV shows can have some interesting segments with celebrities, especially when there's the language barrier. Justin made an appearance on one of Germany's most popular television shows in 2011 a deal-making show called *Wetten Dass...?*, betting that he could finish solving this Rubik's cube. Opposite: Justin takes a minute to pat Barrancas, one of the two mascots of the Spanish TV show *El Hormiguero*, on the head. A popular destination for American stars, Justin charmed the studio audience in Madrid and made himself even more popular in the country, despite the language barrier.

With his sudden rise in fame, Justin needed to let the world know exactly who Justin Bieber is. Starting with his ever-popular YouTube channel, the singer began to make his presence felt, quickly adding an immensely popular Twitter account to his social media empire.

The mainstream media all wanted a piece of the young superstar as well, so Justin began appearing on just about every show under the sun. *Lopez Tonight, Ellen, The Today Show, Good Morning America,* and *Chelsea Lately* were among the shows that on which Justin appeared in the wake of *My World,* with his live performances on other shows more than doubling the total of appearances he made in front of the cameras. He even had his first acting turn in 2009, appearing in an episode of *True Jackson, VP.*

All of this media attention was helping Justin's fan base grow at an even faster rate as the major overnight success story continued. As 2009 came to a close, Bieber

solidified his superstardom when he met President Barack Obama at a Christmas concert, adding the White House to the list of households with Beliebers.

Justin continued his march into 2010 by presenting an award at the Grammys just three months after the release of his debut album. He was already one of the most popular artists in the country and his singles kept on charting. *My World* was expanded into a full-length album called *My World 2.0* in January 2010 and debuted at the top of the Billboard album chart, making Justin the youngest male solo act to top that chart. Its biggest single, "Baby," peaked in the top five and was Justin's top hit to date.

All of a sudden, Bieber was everywhere. This was obviously no flash in the pan—he was selling records at a pace nearly unseen in the digital era. The television appearances kept on coming and Justin continued to charm everywhere he went, including a memorable guest turn on *Saturday Night Live*. After a tour in support of Taylor Swift it seemed

Justin's tours take him all over the world, and this has made him an international superstar. He made a splash after landing in Europe, with throngs of fans selling out arenas all over the continent and screaming as loud—if not louder— than their American counterparts.

like Bieber was ready for just about anything.

Having conquered the media at home, Justin set out on his first world tour, headlining the My World Tour. The most in-demand celebrity in the world was finally heading out on the road for real.

After storming though nearly every major city in the United States and Canada, it was time for Justin to finally go international. He headed to Europe, starting in England and Ireland before making his way to the continent. It should not have been a surprise that Justin was selling out arenas all over Europe, but what was amazing was the scope of the crowds. Thousands of fans turned up to follow Justin's every move despite his never having been there before. The crowds were just as rabid, maybe even louder than the fans back home. France, Germany, the Netherlands, Spain, and Italy all came out in force for Bieber, making him feel right at home.

Asia and Australia followed for Justin, where again massive

Justin's *Never Say Never* was as big a hit abroad as it was at home, bringing in millions of dollars from box offices around the world. The movie saw a European premiere after its regular debut in Hollywood, and here Justin can be seen passing out tickets to lucky fans in the crowd in Paris so that they can enter the premiere and see the movie.

crowds turned out to see the superstar who had never set foot in their countries before. The world simply wanted more of Justin and he had to give it to them.

He went back into the studio to start recording once again and turned his focus to production work on something begun during his tour: a movie. Part biography and part concert film, his project called *Never Say Never* was a bold move for someone just a year into his career. There was little doubt, however, that it was going to be a hit. Everything Bieber has touched so far, after all, has been gold.

Justin's movie was a hit worldwide, and Bieber traveled the world to promote it. In all, the film has grossed nearly $100,000,000 and is the most successful concert movie since 1984. Once again, Bieber had made himself into an even bigger star.

As 2011 wore on following his movie, Justin saw himself pick

Very popular in France as well as French Canada, Justin owes some of his fame in those parts of the world to his French roots. His mom, Pattie, is French Canadian and Justin has spoken French from an early age, even taking a tough school program that uses the language nearly exclusively. Whenever he wins an award in the country or speaks to the media, Justin is just as comfortable in his second language as he is in English.

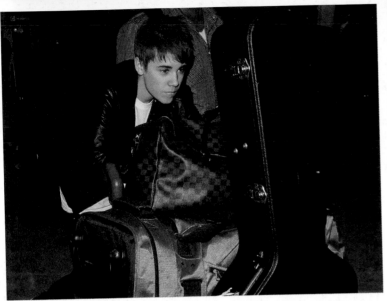

up yet another No. 1 album with *Under the Mistletoe*, his Christmas album. In just two years Justin had written a book, made a movie, been to the top of the album charts three times, been on just about every talk show in the world, and traveled to every continent except Africa and Antarctica. From rags to riches, perhaps no superstar has ever seen a quicker rise than Justin Bieber.

Above: Sometimes being a superstar doesn't matter, and carrying luggage is one of those times. Upon arrival in London in 2011 Justin had to go to work at baggage claim, grabbing his share of the bags his team brought to Europe. Opposite: Justin's European fans are just as dedicated as his fans on this side of the ocean, waiting in line for hours just for the chance to get his autograph.

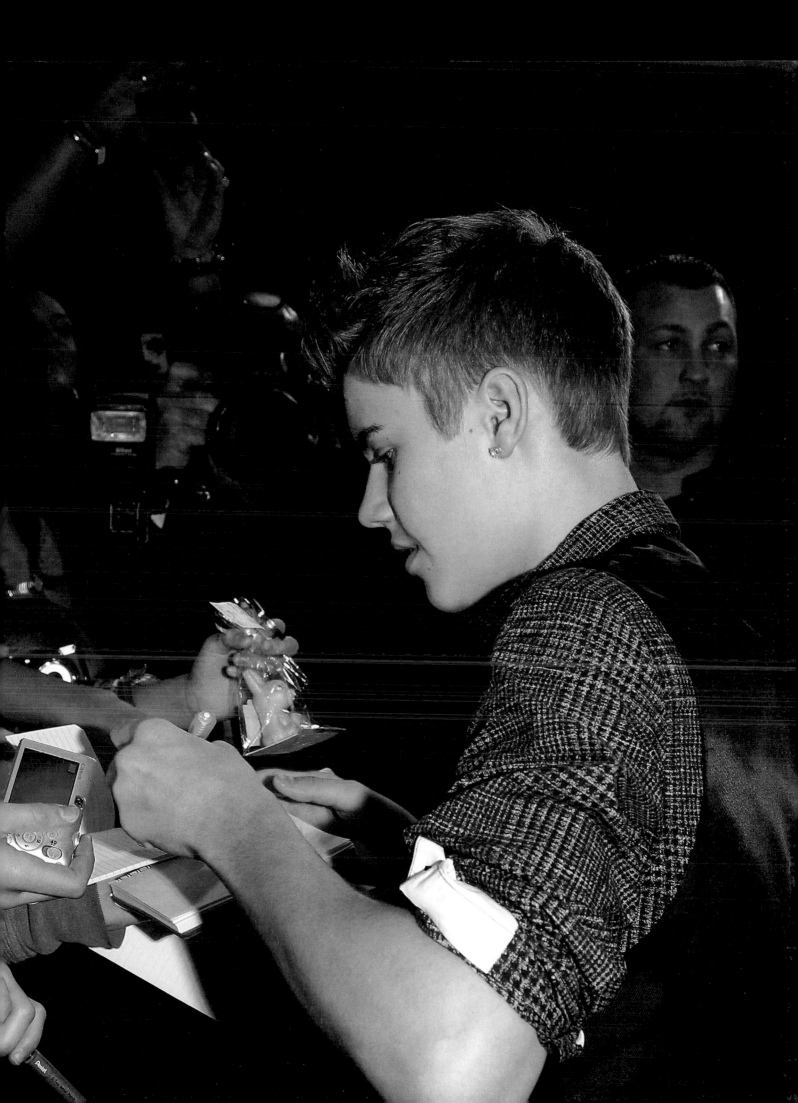

A 21st Century Pop Star

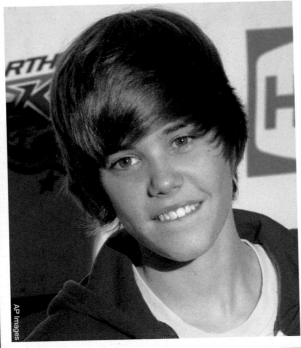

Opposite: Alongside singer Jordin Sparks and funnyman Will Ferrell, Justin arrives for the 2009 Arthur Ashe Kids Day in New York. Justin and Ferrell hit it off, later collaborating on a series of funny videos on FunnyOrDie.com.

It's one of the most famous stories in entertainment in decades—the rags to riches story of a young Canadian singer with a dream and a YouTube account that his mom created for him. The story of Justin Bieber is an underdog story. He wasn't created by a major network, and he didn't have hits handed to him by writers at the studio. He's worked hard to get where he is today, and that spirit has carried him into becoming one of the biggest stars on the planet.

Justin always had a talent for music. His mom, Pattie, raised him in Stratford, Ontario, and the family didn't have much. As a single mom, Pattie had to work hard to provide a decent life for her and her son and one of the things they most enjoyed together was music. Justin began banging on anything he could get his hands on, with early home movies

showing him at the age of five bashing things in time to music playing the background.

This developing ability was noticed by his family, who quickly decided to get Justin some real instruments to play with. He taught himself how to drum, then how to play the piano and guitar. Justin even taught himself how to play the trumpet! It was clear he was a natural at any instrument he tried so when he opened up his mouth to sing for the first time, it was no surprise that it was good. What was surprising was that it was absolutely great.

By the time he was 12, Justin's family knew that he had a rare ability with his musical talents. He entered his first competition, a singing contest put on by the local YMCA. Against much older and more experienced singers Justin wowed the judges and finished second, taking the stage by storm in his first public appearance.

The seed was planted in his head to become a music star. He began busking on the streets of Stratford, earning dollars

A growing part of Justin's musicianship is his skill on the guitar. Already an accomplished player of the instrument, Justin used part of 2009 to make appearances with just him and his guitar, silencing many critics and showing off his all-around musical ability.

Taking Times Square by storm, Justin performs at Tiki Rocks The Square for the Children's Miracle Network at the Hard Rock Cafe in September of 2009. Justin has long been a supporter of children's charities, and the Children's Miracle Network is an organization close to his heart.

here and there but mostly just doing what he loved—playing music. His mom was very proud of everything he had done and wanted to share his skills with family and friends so one day she recorded him singing "So Sick" by Ne-Yo and created a YouTube account. The rest is history.

Justin's video quickly picked up several hundred views, prompting Pattie to post more. His popularity was growing—here was a 12-year-old boy singing like a seasoned R&B artist. When music executive Scooter Braun accidentally stumbled across a video of Justin while looking for one of a different singer, he was instantly hooked.

Braun knows talent when he sees it, and he pushed hard to become Justin's manager, saying that the YouTube account was going to be important to the fan base but that Justin should come to Atlanta to record a demo. After much thought, Pattie agreed and Justin was off to the States.

Justin's instant rise to superstardom is one of the quickest success stories in the history of the music business. In September 2009 Justin's visit to New York saw him followed by an army of screaming fans, a reception not seen for an entertainer in years. Here, Justin looks out at the crowd while appearing at a Nintendo Wii event.

AP Images

Justin performs with a cast on his foot in New York. While supporting Taylor Swift in London in 2009, Justin fractured his foot on stage but continued to perform, later saying that since he is Canadian he is tough and can power through anything. He didn't miss a show and performed with the hard cast on until his foot completely healed.

Justin arrives for his first Grammy Awards in 2010. He made a splash as one of the presenters at the awards, commenting that he couldn't wait to return to win one. It remains one of the last goals Justin has to accomplish, and fans should be ready for the day he eventually takes home one of music's most prestigious awards.

A week after arriving, Justin sang for an audience that included Usher, who was immediately moved by the young singer. He knew he wanted in on the magic that was about to happen, so he teamed with Braun to manage the young singer while he recorded his first few tracks.

Through his contacts, Usher was able to secure a recording contract for Justin, who soon went into the studio to record his first album. This whirlwind excitement in Atlanta may have been a lot to handle, but Justin handled it smoothly. His record wasn't quite finished yet when his first single, "One Time," dropped in 2009. It was a Top 20 hit in the United States, announcing the arrival of the latest pop icon onto the scene. Justin Bieber was quickly building a juggernaut the likes of which the music industry had never seen before.

His first album, an EP called *My World*, was released in November

He was a musician before he was a singer, after all. Justin takes a turn on the drums during a promotional appearance for Best Buy in 2010. He made a special $5,000 donation to a local high school after the appearance. It's not the first time Justin has played drums live: he made a splash when he performed alongside famed drummer QuestLove and the Roots during an appearance on Jimmy Fallon's show.

of 2009 to much fanfare. Nearly every song on the album, such as "One Less Lonely Girl," became hits when they were released as singles and Justin's charm and good looks made him an instant superstar. Despite selling only in the iTunes store, the singles consistently rose up the charts, making Justin an instant hit maker. The album sold a million copies to go platinum and Justin Bieber was off and running with the whole world in front of him.

Above: Other people in the music industry took notice of Justin right from the start and realized that he was about to be a powerhouse in the business. Near the start of his career he attended a party with Pete Wentz, Krisinia DeBarge, and Kenneth "Babyface" Edmonds. Opposite: He's just three years into his career but there's no doubt that Justin Bieber has changed the face of music. It will be exciting to see what he has up his sleeve in years to come!